UPSKILL

AN OPTIMIZATION-CENTRIC COMPETENCE MANAGEMENT

notionpress
.com

UPSKILL

AN OPTIMIZATION-CENTRIC COMPETENCE MANAGEMENT

ASLAM SHERIEFF J

notionpress.com

Notion Press

Old No. 38, New No. 6
McNichols Road, Chetpet
Chennai - 600 031

First Published by Notion Press 2016

ISBN 978-81-7511-081-6

This book is dedicated to my mentors (Renil Komitla, Rama Kini and Sundar Adityan), friends, colleagues, parents, my wife and kids (Waheeda, Armaan, and Ayaan) without whose support and encouragement I would not have completed this book.

Contents

Acknowledgements

First of all, I would like to express my gratitude to all my mentors in industry, friends, family, customers and colleagues. My thanks to all those who trusted in my abilities and gave me new opportunities which definitely were the triggers to write this book.

Without taking names, I would like to thank each and every one who has helped, supported and encouraged me through this journey, I sincerely thank you all!!!

Thanks to all those who talked things over, read, wrote, offered comments, allowed me to quote their remarks and assisted in the editing, proofreading and design.

Above all, I want to thank my wife, Waheeda and the rest of my family, who supported and encouraged me in spite of all the time it took me away from them.

Foreword

I have over seven years of professional relationship with Aslam. I have known him as very hard working, a passionate and meticulous individual who has taken every challenge in his stride to produce meaningful outcome through his result-oriented drive and approach. His need of the hour presence and the confidence that he has given to the management with his can-do attitude is commendable. What he has captured in "Upskill" is a conglomerate of thoughts and challenges that are running through the minds of executives of small, mid and large-sized companies in services and product space. While working with Aslam in Paxterra Solutions [now called Terralogic Inc.], we had seen these challenges together when we did recruitment at different levels starting from college graduates to senior members of the team.

The competency gaps that surface during the inception of the career after graduating from a certain college, are carried by the individuals organization to organization lead to an *avalanche-effect* where executives find it difficult to fill key positions in their charter given that they do not feel confident as the number of years of experience does not reflect the potential candidate's exploratory mind-set and the knowledge that he/she might have amassed over the period of their professional history.

The solution that Aslam has proposed, which is working really great for us today, is a one stop fix to arrest the competence leakage/management right at inception, and taking that study to apply into different levels in the professional career to reduce these gaps for individuals to give better output to the company where they will be delivering their services.

For any individual or executive who is striving to identify a gap, arrest those gaps, learn and evolve as better individuals or have a team of productive, passionate individuals, this book would be a must read.

Thank you

Rama Kini
[CEO Medkumo
Software Solutions Pvt. Ltd.]

There is a crying need for talent in the industry today. How to source, acquire, develop, retain and grow talent in organizations is a million dollar question. This question is giving sleepless nights to CEOs, CXOs, business and HR leaders. Today organizations are under extra-ordinary pressure to create unique customer experiences through products and solutions of superior quality delivered at a speed faster than that of their customers. But isn't it a herculean task? To respond to this challenge organizations today need CAPABILITY. In other words, they need people who have the right knowledge and skill-set.

Some of the knowledge used by professionals today was never taught to them in the universities where they studied. A lot of knowledge they are going to use a decade from now doesn't even exist today. The pace at which current knowledge is getting obsolete and new knowledge is being created is mind-boggling. Individuals and organizations that learn faster than the rate of change around them are going to survive in the 21st century.

Why is the pace of change so swift? Well, primarily because organizations are trying to outwit each other in technology adoption and deployment. Technology is transforming our personal and social lives today in an incredible manner. But there is a flipside to it also. Technology is slowly replacing human beings at the workplace, in factories, in farm-lands and so many other places. Many of the transactional, low skilled jobs like office secretary, accountants, teller clerks, call center agents, translators, interpreters etc. have already been taken away by machines. Now many of the white collar and blue collars jobs are under threat. In China, the first robot-only factory is being built in Dongguan city. The factory aims at reducing their current workforce by 90%. This change is not restricted to manufacturing industry alone. According to a study, Automation will displace 22.7 million US jobs across industries by 2025. What is in store for our graduates who are emerging from our educational institutions every year?

Our educational institutions churn out millions of professional and general graduates and post-graduates every year. Many of them achieve academic excellence by scoring highly in the exams. Students in professional institutions score up to 99.99%. However, the pertinent question is: Does academic excellence often translate into professional excellence? Well, had that been the case, most toppers in our B-Schools and Engineering Colleges would have become corporate CEOs. In organizations, it's not only the IQ or Technical skills that is required. Other factors like Emotional Quotient (EQ), Social Quotient (SQ), Values, Beliefs, Attitude, Knowledge, Family, Culture and upbringing, also have its significance. Ability to see beyond the obvious, ability to work with people, ability to deal with ambiguity, social intelligence etc. are critical competencies which are essential but rarely taught in our colleges and universities. This has created a talent crunch in the industry. The talent crisis is not just restricted to fresh University graduates entering into the corporate world. Today thousands of employees in their mid-career stage are becoming job-less primarily because their skill-set have become obsolete.

The aforesaid examples expose the talent crisis prevalent in our country as well as across the world today. Moreover, these examples clearly demonstrate that our corporate, business and political leaders are clueless about this crisis. The book **Upskill - Optimization - Centric Competence Management by Aslam Sherieff J** comes as a breath of fresh at this critical juncture in the corporate and business history. Aslam deals in the crucial aspects of competency management including identification of business needs, identification of competency gaps, closure of gaps, evaluation of progress etc. According to him competency management is a cyclic process. He explains teach phase of competency management through real examples, repeatable, replicable, scalable frameworks, methods and tools. This book is going to be very helpful to corporates, business houses and educational institutions. I urge upon you to read this book and immensely benefit from it.

Surya Prakash Mohapatra
Senior Management Professional and
Industry Thought Leader

Feedback About the Book

The ideas of the gap between academics and industry experts are not new, but at the same time the new steps initiated by J. Aslam Sherieff may definitely lead to bridge that gap between academics and industry experts. Author constructs the high-level framework concepts in systemic manners and presents key issue related to technology and written in well-spoken language with useful illustration, examples and exercises in each chapter.

The industry questions towards competency blocks are: How do you define the skills, behaviors, and attitudes that workers need to perform their roles effectively? How do you know they are qualified for the job? In other words, how do you know what to measure? In this book the first two chapters i.e. 'Understanding Competency and Optimizations' and "Understanding Competency Gaps Through Industry Perspective" provides the quick answers to above questions explore the various tasks and challenges faced by the industry.

In Chatpter-3, The author proposed the overlapping or hybrid model, which highlights competency lacking areas of traditional model and their possible corrective actions from hiring to onboarding process. This is an interesting research area where huge gap needs to be identified and rectified as per growth in IT. The measurement techniques are provided in chapter-4. No doubt about this techniques, but need more validation and verification from academics and industry experts.

Over all, this pioneering book provides the roadmap to help all of us to have the challenging dialogues that contribute to multicultural understanding this book fulfills few of the gap between academic and industry in competency and optimizations techniques. It would be appreciating if the book has possible case studies examples from few companies. This book is a must-read for students, academics, researchers and Industry experts to understand the various aspects of multi-skill plan, design, development, practice, implement and make further improvement etc.

Dr. K.Gowthaman
Deputy Director (Training & Development),
Inter University Consortium,
Indira Gandhi National Open University (IGNOU),
New Delhi 110068.

"Every time I got bored with a role I changed my boss (and not the organization). Changing boss to me represented disrupting the why, what and how of my work. And it enhanced my knowledge and skills as an individual. In this book, Aslam, presents some answers as to how individuals and organizations could determine their competency level and optimize it to further the organization's mission. Aslam's approach of using a Knowledge and Skill level graph to map competence is something refreshing to read. Also there are some interesting suggestions on Industry-Academic collaborations in up-skilling campus hires, Industries setting up centers of excellence in Universities and Faculty competency improvement programs. Overall a good read."

Sunil Prabhakaran, Co-Founder, Whenda.com

Competency Building Blocks

The objective of competency building blocks shown in Figure 1.A is to represent the high-level idea on how competency management is organized in this book for easy understanding and moreover practising.

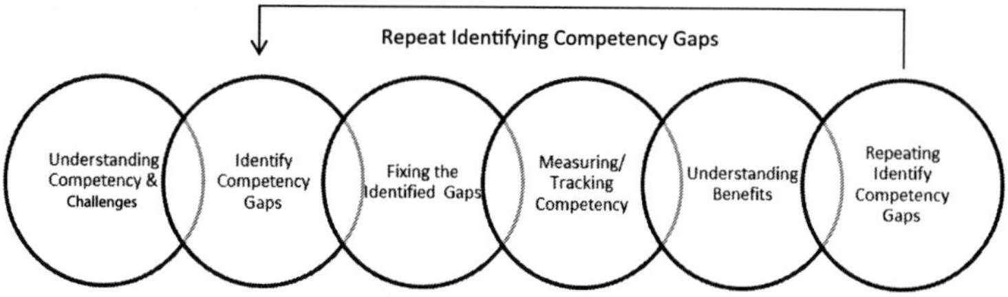

Figure 1.A

Each of the above stages plays a vital role in one's career development phase. Be it a person employed by an organization or a fresh recruit from college or university, they have to go through the above competency building blocks in today's dynamic world to carve a successful career.

Hence, it's recommended that each building block is understood in detail and practised to scale greater heights in career.

CHAPTER

1 Understanding Competency and Optimization

Introduction

Competency today is one of the key focus areas of organizations across the globe. It is highly unlikely, in this day and age, that we'd see a corporate presentation which does not stress the importance of competency across all verticals and industries. The complexity of, and constant need for evolution and innovation in technology today demands a constant improvement in competency levels of technology professionals and SMEs within any technology-oriented business endeavour.

A dynamic and ever-challenging market, characterized by cut throat competition and limited or hard to get resources, further dictates a need for not just intelligent or seasoned professionals, but stalwart individuals with the sufficiency of knowledge and skills that enable them to act responsibly in a wide variety of complex situations.

Along with competency, today organizations face another desperate need for optimization. Organizations are constantly required to operate by finding alternatives with the most cost-effective and/or highest achievable performance under various given constraints. This is achieved by maximizing desired operating factors and minimizing the undesired ones. This is where optimization becomes undeniably important.

Any organization, claiming or hoping to possess a well-rounded and competent workforce/work culture, will make it a point to invest the time and effort required to achieve such optimization.

With the above introduction, let us begin to look at the definition of competency and optimization. As such there are various definitions; I have decided to reuse few of existing definitions.

Definition:

"***Competence*** is the ability of an individual to do a job properly. A competency is a set of defined behaviors that provide a structured guide enabling the identification, evaluation and development of the behaviors in individual employees" – Definition from Wikipedia.

"***Optimization*** in simple terms - To make as perfect or effective as possible. One more way to define optimization could be finding an alternative with the most cost effective or highest achievable performance under the given constraints."

> *Identifying Competency Gaps is an on-going effort and has to be repeated often ...*

Competency includes key elements such as skill and knowledge, which we will discuss more in detail in coming chapters. So, let us park the two elements for now and explore some of the current challenges that the industry faces.

Challenges Faced – Industry Perspective:

- Multi-Skilled Talent Pool
- Value-Additions
- Comprehensive Thinking-Big Picture
- Competency Gaps
- Adapting to Dynamic Changes
- Upskill to Technology Trends
- Understanding Quality and Performance Impacts
- Salary Driven vs. Growth Driven
- Be at comfort zone
- Passion For Technology

Multi-Skilled Talent Pool

A businessman running his own small business often does not get the luxury to hire as many people as he ideally wants for executing his day-to-day needs and requirements. Hence, by nature he gets to handle every aspect of his own business making him multi-skilled or multi-talented in his own domain or business.

With the change of business dynamics, organizations on a global basis are pushed towards transformation, upskilling employee pool and adopt newer fast-paced technologies to ensure that they get upper edge in new business wins or to sustain existing business. This brings in the need for multi-skilled talent pool. Organizations globally are looking at catalysts among employee pool that could adapt quickly, think on their feet and competently perform duties often beyond their defined roles & responsibilities.

Being multi-skilled makes an individual confident and upbeat about the new trends and technology, which in the IT world will help increase his/her age of retirement from the field. Hence, it's evident that multi-skilled talent pool is one of the biggest challenges faced by industry today, and we will see in the following chapters how industry and academics can jointly handle this challenge and convert the people either in organization or colleges/university into a simple businessman who is multi-skilled by nature.

> *It's the need of the hour requirements that defines current employee pool and new hires to be multi-skilled ...*

Value-Additions

Often we hear this question from managers and above – Where is value addition?

Some years ago, when my manager walked in for a meeting and talked, motivated about bringing value-additions into projects, it was something new and interesting for me. I had a detailed discussion and tried to understand what value addition is all about, how it's different from deliverable and inputs on how to find a value addition (the secret method). Then realized over a period that there is no secret method or model, it's how deep you are in your thought process, ability and how strong on the subject that you are dealing with. Once I understood the basics, I started practising the same over the years till date and still trying to see if my thoughts and actions can bring some value addition to organizations, teams and customers.

When we look at the industry today, its bit worrying; the fact that engineers today are not getting a chance to follow the secret method that I mentioned above, which is the art of practising and then adding value. Factors such as lack of competence and mind-set – salary driven vs. growth driven also play a vital role in impacting overall value addition. We will look at the factors which are also part of our challenges list separately. However, the reader needs to keep in mind that these factors and challenges are inter-related and nested.

Value Addition is an art which can be achieved only through practise...

Comprehensive Thinking-Big Picture

One of the common challenges that industries face today from both employee community and new recruits is "Lack of Knowledge on Big Picture." For any strategic decisions taken at the organization level, customer game plans, team objectives/strategies are objective driven. Until teams are completely aware and understand the objectives the purpose is not solved, rather partial-understanding creates assumptions which not necessarily have to be correct in all instances.

It's very much required that employees at various levels within an organization understand the big picture of projects and teams. This would ensure that not just leadership or core teams but all employees are aware of the big picture which would change organizations from good to great!!!

Taking organization from good to great indeed should be all employee strategy and not just leadership team...

Competency Gaps

Thanks to growing business needs and competition. Back then people had to build competence in an area as a first step, then thoughts moved around how they could build a career on top of it and then finally carve a growth path. Today, as soon as an engineer gets a job he or she does not get enough time to build-on the required competence; it's all in a hurried state. People do not sustain themselves enough in one particular job to learn it completely; hence, the gap in competence is moved from one organization to another organization.

This carry-forward of competence gaps from one organization to another is not a good practice in any industry, the reason being these gaps will directly impact the quality of deliverables and key performance indicators.

Competency gaps need to be identified and fixed with improvement plan and timeline...

Adoption of Dynamic Changes

Dynamic changes specific to technology trends, job requirements, customer requirements, stakeholders requirements and change requests have become common today. Now, what is left will be to see how an employee or a new recruit responds to these changes.

An employee or new recruits' responses to dynamic changes are very important. These dynamic changes directly relate to the morale and motivation of the employee. Hence, this becomes a compelling challenge to be dealt very carefully by leadership teams across the organization.

Adapting to dynamic changes or not is individual choice...

Upskill to Technology Trends

Technology, in the last two or three years, has drastically changed and trends that we see today in communication, application development and mobility vertical (to name a few) are creating new innovation re-defining the way we operated few years ago.

With this change, a question to employee or new recruit aspiring to switch jobs will be willingness and interest towards upskilling one's technical knowledge or upgrading oneself. Practising upskill will enable an individual to become more robust and potential contender for new growth opportunities within the organization. Finally, not upskilling to latest technology or trends will result in competency gaps, which will start widening as the year progresses. Moreover, upskilling needs to be looked at as an on-going process for employees and new recruits.

Upskill are not burden, Rather they help you stay in business for some more time...

Understanding Quality and Performance Impacts

How are organizations today measured by their investors/customers/stakeholders? An obvious answer will be the performance of their products, sales or services and how happy a customer is. Given that we understand organizations are measured by performance, next question that comes to mind is how engineering teams are measured today?

Does their performance impact overall competence? The reason for me to ask quite a few questions is due to the fact that quality and performance of engineering teams today are measured based on a variety of data points, computations, questions, progress made and much more.

Hence, it's required for the employee, new recruit or fresh graduate to understand what are the quality standards of an organization, standards being followed by their teams and how the performance of team/individual is measured and what are the parameters used.

What we see in today's engineering teams are managers or supervisors computing and sharing quality and performance measures to the management in monthly review meetings and improvements/actions derived as a part of the action plan as an outcome of the review meeting. Now, how much knowledge a team member has to the data being shared, making some inferences derived from the review meeting debatable. Now where is competence being discussed in this challenge is something you will be having in mind by now. Competence is an important performance or quality indicator which is always taken for evaluation and measurement in review meetings. If you are a manager/supervisor and assuming that you do not add competence in your review meetings, then it's time to revisit and see how you can add the competence also in your reviews.

A team manager or supervisor shares the teams' competence for a given period of time and measures the improvement of the team or individual and what he or she lacks and action plans to improve and fix. Hence, understanding the quality and performance indicators are most important factors and it needs to reach each and every employee of an organization and teams.

Employee/New hires/Fresh Grad should ask their managers or supervisors how quality, performance of their team and their work is being measured?

Salary Driven vs. Growth Driven

This is one of the important factors impacting competence today and in future. This challenge is more to deal with the "Mindset" of an individual. A growing start-up culture, growing business demands and needs can be thanked for the same. Winning the competition, time to market is the key here, and organizations are ready to afford a high price being offered to an individual. While it's a good sign for the industry, an individual with the right skillset will get the right opportunity to grow in career. However, there are no perfect ways of working. Observation is that even an individual without enough skills with competence gaps gets from one job to another job. Hence, the gap in competence is carried from one organization to another organization.

Individual mindset is changing from growth to salary-driven. The key driver "Growth" is not a mantra anymore. Salary has increasingly become a compelling factor for an individual in today's environment. There are various factors for this change, but we will limit our scope just to discuss the change of mindset and how this is becoming one of the important challenges that industry is facing today with respect to competence.

Be at Comfort Zone

This is a common problem that the industry is facing with the mid to senior level employees. People in this bracket have settled contributing in one or more specific technology. Some of the above challenges that we discussed such as adapting to dynamic change, upskilling, mindset and more are seen primarily due to the fact "Be at comfort zone." Only a handful of people in the above bracket are ready to move towards new technology, trends and upskilling.

If existing employees or new recruits are reluctant to move towards taking up a new opportunity, he or she decides to stay in a comfort zone, which might, in turn, impact the overall competence of an individual and create a gap at an organization level.

Passion for Technology

It is a straight forward thought – organizations have the objective to build and grow employees who have the passion for technology. But the challenge is in the commitment-level and percentage of involvement or passion for technology. If he or she is not passionate enough about technology, his or her deliverables will not be of great quality, and there will be direct performance degradation seen, which will bring in further competency gaps and affect the overall productivity of a team. Hence, organizations, leadership teams, managers, supervisors, individual employees, new recruits and fresh graduates need to participate in promoting passion for technology.

Employee *Fresh Grads*

Leadership Teams

New hires *Organization*

Passion for Technology is a common objective and all the above are part of this drive.

KEY TAKE AWAY

- Competency Building Blocks
- Understanding Competency And Optimization
- Understanding Challenges Faced
- Promoting Passions Towards Technology

CHAPTER

2 Understanding Competency Gaps through Industry Perspective

Introduction:

In this chapter, we will understand how competency gaps arise, primary reasons, industry expectation and finally how we categorize the gaps. It is important for each and every working professional/new recruit out from colleges to know their respective competency levels and gaps, which will be useful in shaping one's career and bring success.

Let us now explore four major topics which will explain where this competency gap is coming from, what is the gap, why do we see the gap and how do we identify the gap.

- Rapid Build-up and Breakthrough Culture
- Where is the competency gap coming from?
  - Understanding Competency Gap vs. Business Needs
  - What actually is the gap?
- Industry Expectation vs. Academic Knowledge
  - Why do we really see the gap?
- Identify Competency Gaps using Knowledge & Skill Arrow
  - How to identify the gap?

By Understanding this chapter & Practising the approach you will be elevating yourself one level up in your career towards growth path...

Rapid Build-up and Breakthrough Culture

The book *Good To Great* by Jim Collins talks about build-up and breakthrough in detail. The observation that I have made based on current state of the industry is organizations existing (some) and new would like to transform which is healthy, but at "what" pace really matters.

Organizations, today, want to achieve rapid build-up and breakthrough. There are enough justifications and reasons supporting the reason for organizations to follow the "Rapid" culture. Startup ventures are increasing by the day, and they are pressed for time to reach the market or customer in a short span; stakeholders' money is at risk. Organizations need to start raking profits or bring in ROI as soon as possible. Some organizations want to make quick profit and exit.

Ideally, for an organization moving from good to great is a huge transformation and it needs time and effort. While today's organization still wants to achieve build-up and breakthrough culture, the difference is at what speed. To achieve and support the "Rapid" progress there will be various factors which need to be addressed; one such will be competency. The need to quickly adapt and deliver at rapid pace will bring in dynamic changes and upskill on technology. Hence, people who form core teams need to be on top of these changes and upskill themselves on the needed trends/technology.

Hence, it's a kind of evident that the strategy to build and breakthrough at rapid pace indirectly brings in competency gaps, which is the need of the hour and understanding this by existing employees and new recruits from college will help individuals to a great extent to align with prevailing industry trends and culture.

> *An organization strategy to build and breakthrough at "Rapid" pace indirectly will bring in competency gaps...*

Understanding Competency Gap vs. Business Needs

Now that we have seen how an organization strategy of rapid build-up and breakthrough can bring in competency gaps, there are business needs as well which can bring in competency gap. It's important to understand business needs and its relationship with competency.

Again, business needs can come directly from the customers/end users/change in overall business dynamics/change in technology, trends and much more. There are a lot of compelling business needs which calls for upskilling, failing to upskill gives way for competency gaps to arise.

The difference here is the gaps seen through business needs could vary from one group to another. Hence, we need to identify what driver is causing the competency gap.

For example, for some groups, it could be process gaps, for some it could be lack of specific technical expertise.

Hence, spotting the right business need can define the actual gap.

Another way to look at this is, some of the business needs call for upskilling even on every three or six months. Hence, the competency gap coming out of this kind of business needs or scenarios can be seen as an on-going effort and not a one-time effort.

Finding the Competency gap will be an on-going effort...

Industry Expectation vs. Academic Knowledge

In this section, we will explore the expectations from industry with respect to competency vs. academic knowledge. As we are aware, academic knowledge primarily is well-defined and based on certain guidelines and process.

On other side, business dynamics cause fluctuations in industry demands. Industry expectations are based on certain parameters (limited to few parameters) future roadmap of projects, customer expectations and overall business strategy. Based on these parameters, the required competency, skills vary time-to-time. Due to this, there is an expectation difference between what is needed for the industry vs. academic knowledge.

This aspect is debatable. Industries have defined the basic knowledge needed for a specific job requirement, and once resources are on-boarded, they are channelled into learning and development programs which upskill employees, make them ready and acquire needed skills to perform a certain job.

Now we are trying to explore the possibility of optimizing this factor also, if we are optimizing the ramp up or upskilling which happens after employee on-boarding, then there has to be a way to upskill before on-boarding. Now we call this as a competency gap and thereby, the difference seen on competency is something to be understood.

Gone are those days where expectations of industry were bare minimal when hiring an employee. In today's changing world, expectations are increasing which I call changing business dynamics. This is one good way to understand that our basic expectation itself needs to be upskilled, which is coming to terms with the fact that industry needs and academic knowledge have to go hand-in-hand, and there is a need to overlap according to industry trends and changes. Hence, it's required to understand both the industry expectation and what is being offered or gained as a part of academic knowledge.

> *There is a business need for overlapping industry and academics which can solve lot of competency related issues seen today...*

Identify Competency Gaps using Knowledge & Skill Arrow

In the above sections, we have understood various industry perspectives stating the importance or need for competency upskilling time-to-time. Now let us look at ways of identifying the actual competency gap. For this, we will use a simple and effective approach using knowledge and skill arrow. This is not the only approach. There are several approaches being used by industry-experts to identify or measure the gaps, but we will use one of the approaches known as knowledge and skill arrow for our discussion as shown in below Figure 2.A.

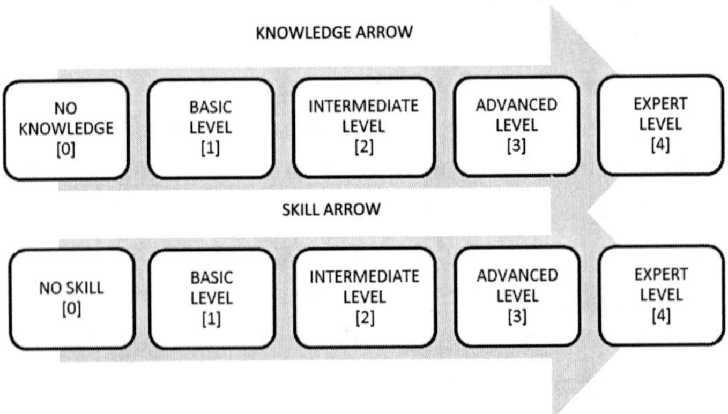

Figure 2.A

Let us look at two key elements that play a vital role in identifying the competency gaps.

- Knowledge
- Skill

Knowledge is conceptual, and skill is knowledge that is applied. With these two basic elements, there are various levels of knowledge and skills used for measuring one's actual state. Let us look at them at length.

Knowledge Levels:

- No knowledge (Rating 0)
- Basic level of conceptual knowledge (Learner Level or Rating 1)
- Intermediate level of conceptual knowledge (Knowledgeable Level or Rating 2)

- ➲ Advanced level of conceptual knowledge (Highly Knowledgeable Level or Rating 3)
- ➲ Expert level of conceptual knowledge (Expert Level or Rating 4)

Therefore, the above levels help us determine the area or the set of areas at which an employee or a new recruit is at. These are only levels which are similar to parameters, we have not yet discussed areas where these will be applied for measuring.

We are trying to make our point that with these levels we can clearly indicate a person's knowledge level.

Skill Levels:

- ➲ No Skill (Rating 0)
- ➲ Basic level of applied knowledge (Basic Level or Rating 1)
- ➲ Intermediate level of applied knowledge (Intermediate Level or Rating 2)
- ➲ Advanced level of applied knowledge (Advanced Level or Rating 3)
- ➲ Expert level of applied knowledge (Expert Level or Rating 4)

The above levels help us determine at which level an employee or a new recruit against skill or applied knowledge stands.

The common practise followed is knowledge measured at a college or with a new recruit and skill is measured at industry. In the case of a lateral employee, he or she will be measured against the skill, which will give us directly the competency gap against his or her skills and job requirement.

For both scenarios, it is important to arrive at a baseline as without baseline measuring does not make sense at all. Hence, organizations or institutions need to conclude on where to get or create the baselines from. There are various ways to create baselines in general. A straight forward approach will be to create baseline during on-boarding of an employee or when hiring a fresh graduate from college(s) can define criteria where to derive the baselines and start measuring from thereon.

Below is an example of how competency is measured, we have considered areas as the parameters which will be used to measure and ratings indicate what is measured and what is required as per the job description. The items that do not meet the required average will fall as competency gaps. Say, if required average for an area is at three, and the measured average is at two, there is a gap between both.

Sample Areas (For Communication Vertical): Inter-Process Communication, Socket Programming, Multithreading, Data Structures, Process-Agile, Perl Scripting.

Example of Competency Baseline									
Resource Details	Group	Area 1	Area 2	Area 3	Area 4	Area 5	Area 6	Area 7	Area 8
Person 1	AA	3	2	3	1.5	2	3	2	2
Person 2	AB	3	3	3	3	3	2.5	2	2
Person 3	AA	3	3	2	3	1.5	1.5	2	1.5
Measured Average		3.00	2.67	2.67	2.50	2.17	2.33	2.00	1.83
Required Average		3	3	3	3	3	3	2	2

Figure 2.B

Classification	Rating
No Skill	0
Basic	1
Intermediate	2
Advanced	3
Expert	4

Figure 2.C

Before we move to the next chapter, it's recommended that readers practise the above gap analysis.

Gap Analysis Practise Example:

Objective: This is to make readers familiar with identifying competency and gaps.

Activity: Readers should try to perform self-assessment on their knowledge and skillset and come up with baseline reports using a simple spread sheet as shown in Figure 2.B & C.

If you are part of the institution and studying: Self-assessment based on knowledge in the domain of interest.

If you are an employee: Self-assessment based on skillset in the domain of work or interest based on future project roadmap or individual roadmap for growth.

Expectations: Once you have completed the above activity, you should have the baseline done based on the category you are presently in. This should fairly give you a good idea of your own competency and the levels you stand at present.

We will see how to use the above baseline and plan the next steps in coming chapters.

KEY TAKE AWAY

- Understanding various industry factors impacting competency
- Understanding knowledge & skill arrow
- Deriving competency baselines
- Identifying competency gaps
- Practise example for self-assessment

CHAPTER

3 Fixing the Identified Gaps

Introduction:

In this chapter, we will learn how to fix the identified gaps. If you have already tried practising assignment no.1 in the above section, then by now you have your competency gaps ready for you. Now in this section, we will explore various approaches to a different community of people who are part of institutions, organizations or technical members belonging to institutions.

Optimization is another area that needs to be discussed. Now in this section, we will see optimization playing a bigger role. Our approaches to fix the identified gaps are optimization centric.

Need for Overlapping/Hybrid Model

In this topic, we will discuss more towards the traditional hiring model which is more to deal with people fresh out from colleges. This may not be applicable directly to lateral hires or employees who move from one organization to the other.

Graduates form the next generation of the resource pool. Hence, we need to look at the commonly-followed model of hiring to on-boarding which we will refer to as traditional model from now on in this book and how this can be improved with the help of a model which we will refer as overlapping or hybrid model.

Let us look at some of the factors which are pushing the need for overlapping or hybrid model compared to the traditional model. Please refer to Figure 3.A below.

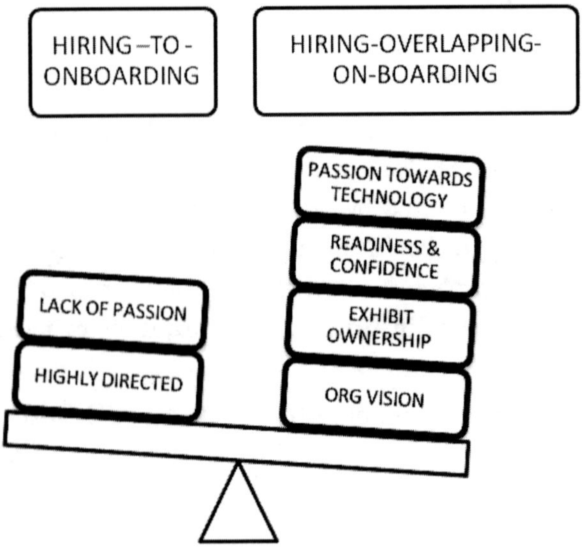

Figure 3.A

Let us explore the factors more in depth.

Traditional Model (Hiring-to-On-boarding)

In this model, which is being commonly used for some years now, one of the key observations is that there is lack of passion in those who are hired and on-boarded. There could be many reasons for this lack of passion at entry-level, but this factor will impact if it is not addressed in a proper way at the root level.

Another factor which impacts is that people who are hired through this model seem to be highly directed. This might not be the case with everyone being hired, but this seems to be increasing day-by-day. Hence, we cannot generalize the models followed by the organization today, but if we look at the overlapping or hybrid model, definitely as a reader you will appreciate the overall weightage of both the models and how they can benefit the community at large.

Overlapping Model (Hiring-Overlapping-On-boarding)

We are trying to optimize the traditional model by bringing in the overlapping in between hiring and on-boarding. As a reader, you might be wondering where we are optimizing? The answer is simple: once hired and on-boarded, organizations spend money, time and effort to get their resource pool ramp up and upskill, now this is where most of the cases such as lack of passion creeps in and they become highly directed.

By bringing in overlapping, organizations can take certain advantage and leverage the ramp up or upskill activity to the source where the resources are hired (institutions or universities) and save money through reducing operational cost, time of the engineering staff and effort.

This overlapping model can increase passion for technology with a visible increase in readiness and confidence among the new recruit. What industry wants is to exhibit more ownership, which is possible through the overlapping model.

Now that we have seen some of the factors representing traditional model and overlapping model and also understood the need for an overlapping model. Let us see how we can overlap between industry and academics.

Overlapping Industry & Academics

How do we really overlap industry and academics? Before we look into the proposed model, we need to understand the fact that this is a collective and collaborated effort between industry and academics hence there is no magic as such in this approach.

This approach will take academics closer to industry and industry will also need to come forward, and rest is how all good overlapping happens giving way to new thoughts and approaches for future.

Let us look at a typical hiring model, which normally will be a selection of a place for hiring along with sorting of the required logistics. Once that is done, the next step will be actual hiring. The step after that will be on-boarding. This third step or phase is where we are proposing the overlapping. Please refer to Figure 3.B.

Now let us look at an overlapping stage in the detailed process. Ideally, once the hiring completion is done, the next step would be to collaborate with intuitions to come up with a model to bring in the various ramp up areas and define milestones for each area with activity to be accomplished, timelines and evaluation criteria. By repeating this for a period defined which could be anywhere ranging from three—eleven months, this is shown in below Figure 3.C. This period can be compared with the time and efforts spend after hiring, on-boarding, and ramp up.

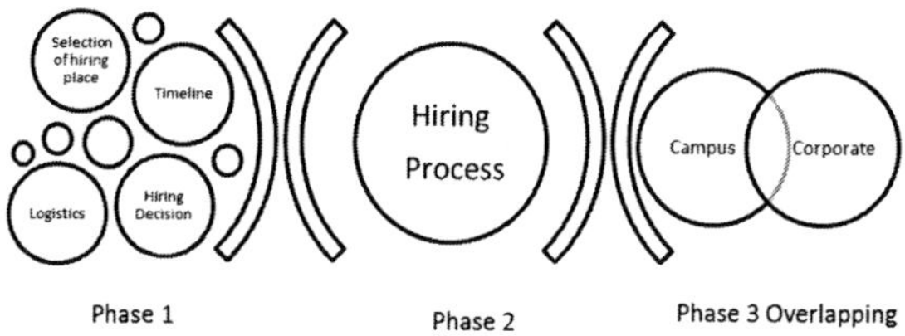

Figure 3.A

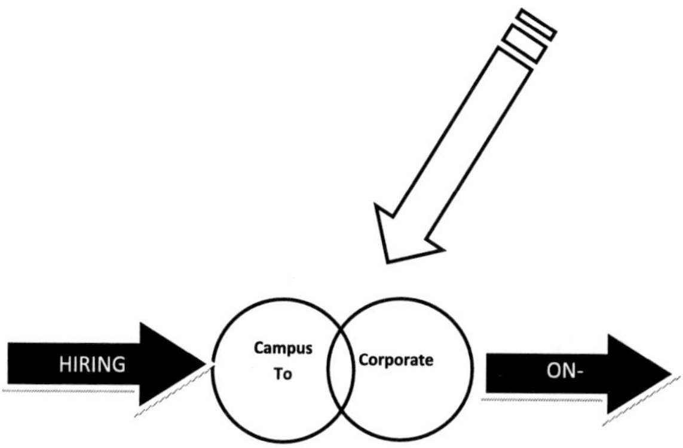

Figure 3.B

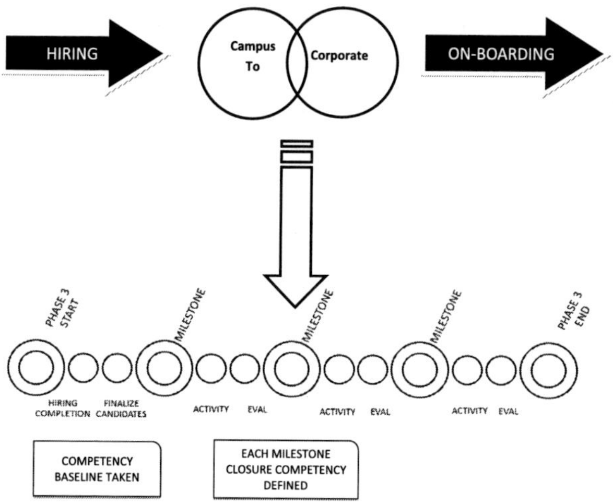

Figure 3.C

By ramping up through various milestones, we are trying to optimize the process at the organization level, thereby, giving the optimizing benefit back to organization bringing institutions closer to industry. Also, if you note the above Figure 3.C, the competency baseline will be taken when phase three begins and also will define what competency is expected at milestones closure. Then, rest is just measuring whether we achieved the planned competency or not.

Let us move ahead and look at collaborative options proposed in this chapter, which can help further to fix the competency gaps seen.

Collaborative Options

There are various collaborative options, we will present few of them which are again optimization-centric approaches.

Collaborated Competency Development:

Institutions today offer a variety of value-added programs for the benefit of the student community. Having surveyed some of the value-added programs, it's observed that the value-added programs enhance or increase the knowledge curve, but they don't really increase skill curve which is required for the industry to a large extent.

Hence, to overcome this and fix the competency gap, it's required that institutions should come forward and adopt the programs which will enhance or improve the skill curve rather than the knowledge curve, in specific. If this is achieved to the fullest, organizations do not have to spend time and effort in ramping up these resources, rather they can begin straightaway with job training. Please refer Figure 3.D.

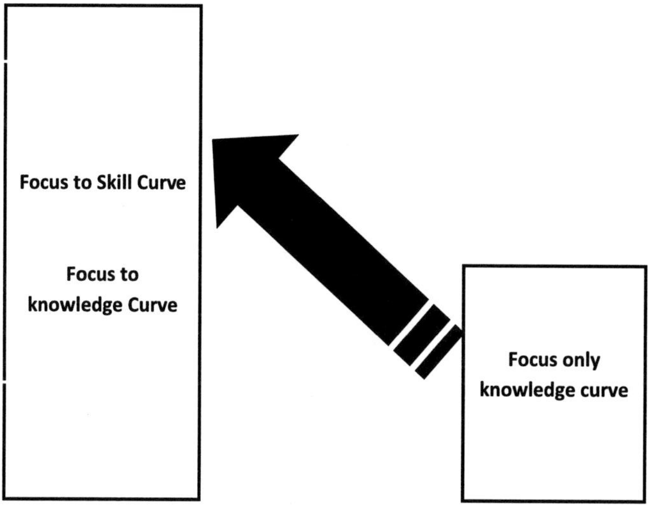

Figure 3.D

Concept of COE (Center of Excellence):

This is not new to the industry. COE has been in practise for some years now and in different capacities. Some organizations have their own COE to funnel the R&D efforts. Then the oblivious question is what difference we are referring here? The COE model that we would like to discuss here is unique. Organizations need to come forward in setting up COE in institutions, which will enable collaborations between industry and academics. Again we need to apply optimization thought here and see how we can leverage the COE for R&D activity, innovation, upskill, ramp up on required technology, proof of concept, joint development projects and joint revenue generation projects and not just limiting to internships.

Organizations should look at COE as an extension of their R&D teams and may consider them as *virtual* R&D teams. These virtual COEs can be further categorized according to business vertical based on industry or any organization business focus areas. This will help scale the organizations from where are today to next level and reduce or control prevailing high resource cost in the market place.

If you look more in depth, you will see that in this approach, we are trying to push key industry demands into COE directly. Ideally the industry demands no longer are a part of the only industry, but it also needs to be a part of COE. The problems should be shared, this thought is the key driver for COE approach. The COE teams should be seen as an extension of the agile and engineering teams as shown in Figure 3.E.

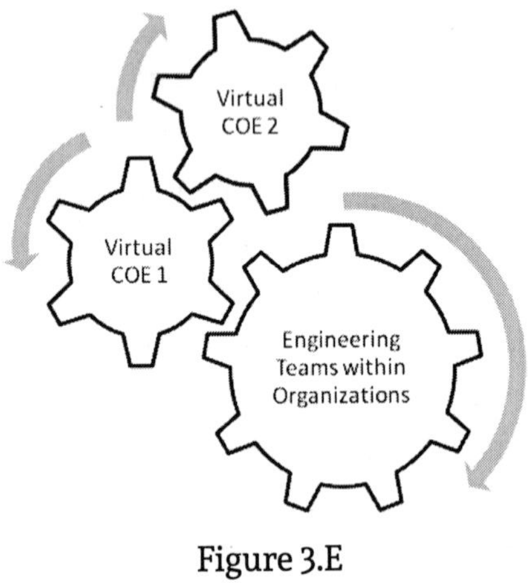

Figure 3.E

Defined Internships:

Are internships and defined internships different? They are similar, but the way it needs to be executed will be slightly different. We will bring optimization thought here. That means we will need to use defined internships, which is leveraging the internships to ramp up or upskill on the industry demanding technology or area of interest where strategically organization is focussing.

This is debatable. The reason some readers might feel that defined internships are followed today, and there is nothing new in thought, even though the defined internships exists today, we don't see people following it 100%, hence, this is one area which needs improvement, which can, in turn, reduce cost, time and effort on the organization front and institutions will be enabled with more meaningful industry demanding trends and technology to focus on.

Optimizing L&D:

How much cost do organizations spend on L&D? It differs from one organization to other, but there is a considerable amount of investment and effort goes into this activity. My question to readers, do we need L&D? Can't employees who are part of the system upskill themselves on upcoming trends and technology based on industry demands and needs?

As we discussed of sharing our key problems with academics, why don't we let employees look upskilling and ramp up by themselves rather providing L&D? May be L&D can be provided for certain soft skills, but when it comes to core technology it would be more useful if we optimize the L&D and let employees take ownership on upskilling themselves. I will leave this topic here for readers to think more and plan.

Faculty Competency Improvement Program:

The faculty members who are part of institutions can play a vital role in some of the collaborated options discussed above such as collaborated competency development program, COE and defined internships. We talked a lot so far on upskilling and ramping up employees and new recruits, but what about faculty members? Are they not an integral part of the system? Yes, if we say they are, then there needs a system in place for them to identify competency and then fix, upskill. There is a lot of opportunity for the faculty member to participate in the above options, it needs some level of planning and mindset to explore and make use of opportunity so as to stay top of new trends and technology.

With this, we conclude in this section where we have discussed in detail various ways of fixing the identified gaps keeping optimization centric. The above topics will bring in real value only when it's practised on an on-going basis.

KEY TAKE AWAY

- Traditional model and overlapping model
- Overlapping industry and academics
- Collaborated competency development
- Collaboration options
- Practising...

CHAPTER

4 Measuring and Tracking Competency

Introduction:

In this chapter, we will learn methods to measure and track the planned competency. As discussed in earlier chapters, the activity of identifying competency is an on-going process, and we discussed various perspectives, factors and ways to identify the competency gaps. In this section, we will understand why measuring and tracking is important and how do we really achieve it.

Need for Improvement Plan

Let us start with a question, what will be the next step once we identify the competency gap? It will be to look at ways to fix the gap; the next question will be how do we fix? The answer is through an improvement plan. An identified gap should have an improvement plan clearly defining the areas of improvement needed, moreover without an improvement plan measuring or tracking competency is of no use.

It's sort of action plan to fix the gaps seen. As such there is no template for deriving improvement plan, but what would help is a detailed plan. This improvement plan needs to be revisited after a certain interval of time to measure the performance against the plan.

Timeline to Achieve

Timeline to achieve goes hand-in-hand with an improvement plan. A plan without a timeline to achieve is again of no use. Ideally, improvement plan should have a detailed plan and timeline to achieve or complete for each time in the plan.

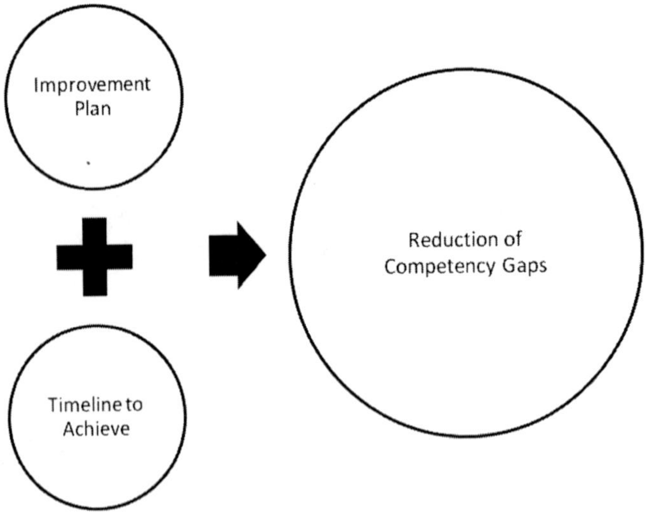

Figure 4.A

Once the timeline has arrived, the feedback needs to be taken, and again the competency needs to be measured. Once measured it needs to be compared to see if there is an improvement or real progress seen. If yes, then the model is working as expected and the end result will be similar to Figure 4.A, ideally reduction of competency gaps. If not, there is something seriously missing, it can be gap itself not identified properly or not so effective improvement plan.

Various Depiction model

There are various ways to depict the competency gaps and measure them. We will show few examples of measuring competency.

1. Using Competency Spider – Where you measure against the required average.

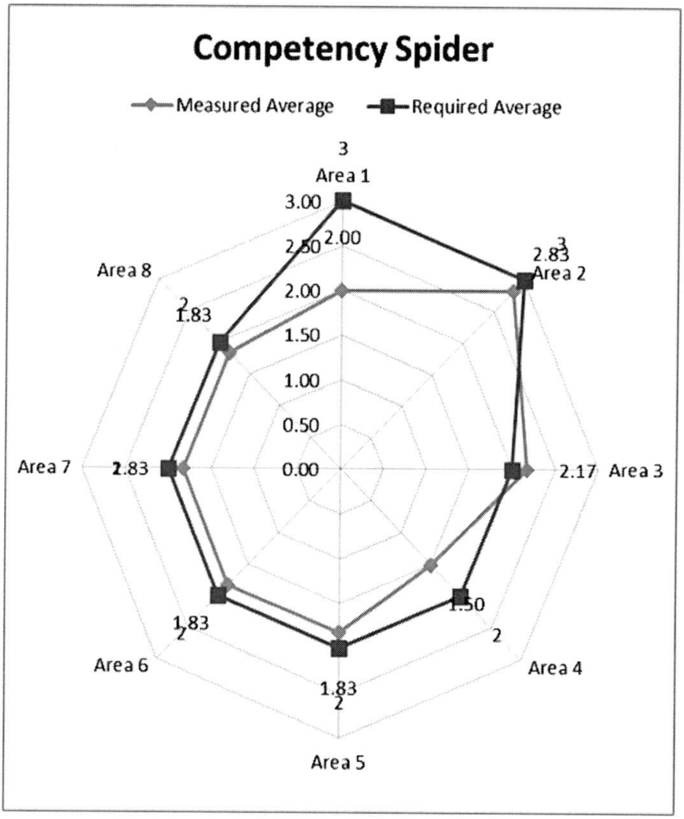

Figure 4.B

2. Compare using Competency Spider – Comparing 2 spiders taken at different intervals helps measure improvement over competency.

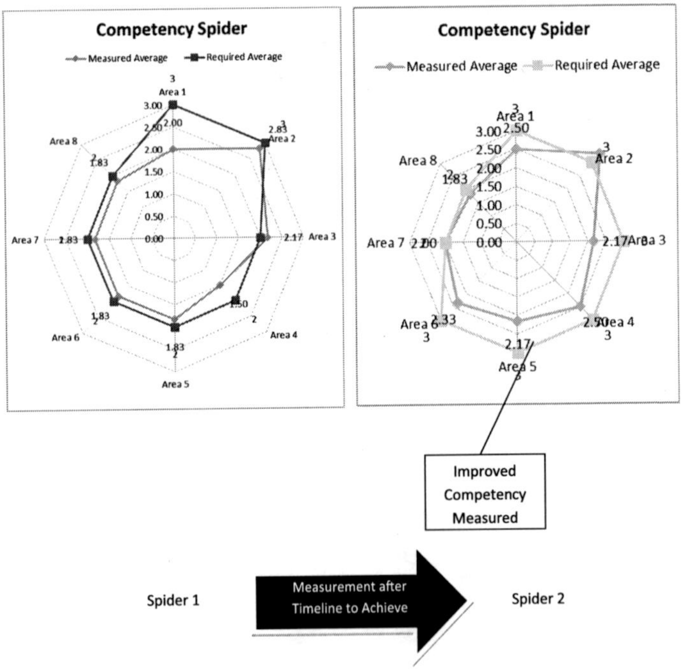

Figure 4.C

3. Comparing with Business Needs

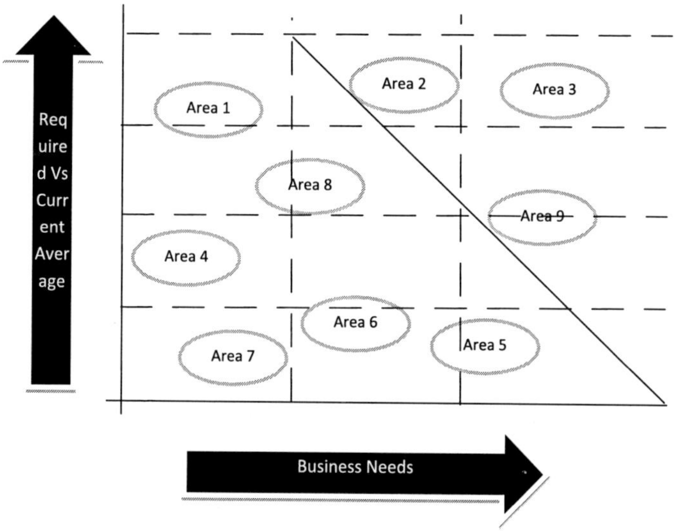

4. Simple Gap Matrix Representation.

Simple Gap Matrix			
Competency	Required	Current	Gap
Area 1	5	3	2
Area 2	5	2	3
Area 3	4	3	1
Area 4	3	3	0
Area 5	4	4	0
Area 6	4	4	0
Area 7	4	2	2
Area 8	3	1.5	1.5

Repeat Measurement

Finally, the measurement and tracking process need to be repeated again after a certain period (interval) of time. Measuring and tracking will be an on-going effort. That is, when the teams will ideally become effective.

KEY TAKE AWAY

- Need for improvement plan
- Timeline to achieve
- Competency spider
- Competency spider comparison
- Comparing competency against business needs
- Repeat measurement

CHAPTER

5 Benefits of Optimization-Centric Competency Management

Introduction:

There are various benefits one can reap following the approaches discussed in the earlier chapters. Organizations worldwide are looking today to optimize the overall cost & resources. Hence, the approaches designed and shared in this book are optimization centric.

As we have repeatedly been saying in this book, the approaches need to be practised to obtain the benefits. Some of the key benefits are listed below in Figure 5.A. Let us now understand the benefits bit more in depth.

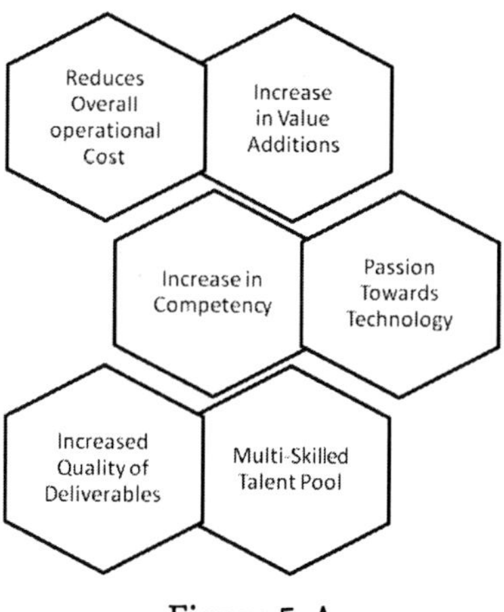

Figure 5. A

Benefits of Optimization-Centric Competency Management

Reduces Overall Operations Cost:

Organizations around the world today are very keen on resource utilization. Any form of optimization which can bring in benefits and reduce operational cost in right perspective is appreciated. This is applicable to industries and the academia also. Hence, the approaches, thoughts discussed in this book when practised will help bring in overall operational cost reduction.

Organizations can reap direct benefits by leveraging and overlapping with college/university to help build required technology ramp up ahead in the game. Factors discussed here are limited, but the scope of where it can be applied or how is plenty. Hence, we will leave it over here for readers/practitioners for more brainstorming and exploration.

Increase of Value Addition:

One of the key benefits of competency management is that it will give way to an increase in overall value additions. Value additions are key to any organization for its growth strategy or for an individual for his or her own growth. Value additions are possible when there is an increased passion towards technology. Both of these are inter-related for all reasons they go in synchrony.

Increase of Quality of Deliverable:

This is one of the important business aspects. Business and its stakeholders are more interested in the performance of organizations or products or projects and quality. Quality can help get more business, sustain the existing business, and create brand value and reputation. Ideally following competency management system approaches organizations or individuals will observe the quality of deliverables getting better or efficient.

Multi-Skilled Talent Pool:

Its need of the hour, we need multi-skilled talent pool in today's scenario. Hence, creating multi-skilled talent pool within organization or outside the organization is strategy decision. But organizations going forward will start looking for multi-skilled talent in an individual. Hence, employees of new recruit or people moving from one job to another or student community, elicit the fact that becoming multi-skilled in their domain is a necessity, so they stay in business for more time.

With this, we have reached close to wrapping up this book, and I would like to recommend readers to start looking at how you can start practising some of the approaches discussed in this book for creating a better competent talent pool for future.

Epilogue

Frequently Asked Questions

Q. What is the significance of using knowledge and skill arrow?

A. We have taken knowledge and skill arrow for the very good reason that it can clearly depict what is acquired at a college/university level and what is acquired on the job as an employee. It helps state which level one is since there is level ranging from 0—4. It will be helpful in assessing one's level.

In addition, the arrow shows the difference and importance of skills which are needed or expected by industry and comparing with knowledge gives a clear indication that there will always be a gap, and one has to identify and fix them, which will be an on-going process in this changing dynamic world.

Q. How important is the baseline for measuring one's competency?

A. Any measurement if done against baseline will be helpful. Baseline gives an idea of where one stands and when further measurements are taken, then it's compared with baselines and shows the improvement one is making and which will be shown in the reduction of competency gap.

Q. Is this the perfect model for measuring competency?

A. No. There are plenty of ways to measure the competency, which used by industry experts today, this is just one way, and intention is to make readers start practising one or other method which is used for measuring competency. The objective is to make people aware of competency, its importance and how it can add value to their career.

Q. Who gives required average?

A. Its straight forward it comes from project stakeholders, customers, internal teams, supervisor, and managers.

Q. Who gives measured average?

A. It comes from the project stakeholders, feedbacks, customers, feedbacks against the objectives set, observations from roles & responsibilities set.

Q. In terms of colleges/universities, knowledge areas will be available, but areas specific to skills might not be available, how will this be handled?

A. This needs overlapping both industry and colleges/ university for identifying the required skillset along and plan to address the same.

Q. Can improvement plan bring in an increase of competency?

A. Improvement plan cannot alone bring an increase in competency. The other depending factors such as timeline to achieve, measuring, monitoring and repeating need to be followed to achieve better results.

Forward Thinking Summary

Below is a forward thinking summary rather than summarizing the key topics discussed in the book.

- Upskill – An Optimization-Centric Competency Management System is still an area which can be refined and more working models and approaches can be brought in. Hence it's a new area open for further research.
- Competency Management System taking place in main stream education, where student community is well versed in understanding how these approaches/models can bring in benefit well in advance, so preparation can begin proactively.
- The concept of more than one Virtual COE which will look like an extension to the core teams (within organizations) can bring lot of value additions and help create innovations and value additions.
- Virtual COE can help organizations/college/universities scale and growth faster adopting new technology and trends.
- Practising these approaches can lead to new working models and further can lead towards optimization of the approaches discussed in this book.